W9-DBX-028

40 Soul-Stretching Conversations

* * *

writing
a spiritual journal
with
JOAN CHITTISTER

Benetvision
Erie, Pennsylvania

Benetvision
355 East Ninth Street
Erie, PA 16503-1107

Phone: 814-459-5994   Fax: 814-459-8066
www.joanchittister.org
benetvision@benetvision.org

Benetvision: Research and Resources
for Contemporary Spirituality is a ministry of the
Benedictine Sisters of Erie.

Excerpted from *Called to Question: A Spiritual Memoir*
by Joan Chittister, published by Sheed & Ward
(Rowman & Littlefield)

Cover design: Judy Allison

ISBN: 978-1-890890-97-1

15 16 17 3 2 1

* * *

FORWARD

Over the years I've come to a new awareness:
There is such a thing as a spiritual life
that is deeper—
and truer to the demands of the world around it—
than simply the routines of religious discipline.
And I wanted it.

To chart my way through the dark waters of life
that were not aways navigable by given standards,
I began to keep a spiritual journal—
a kind of dialogue with the ideas of other writers
whose concerns had also been spiritual,
whose musings were also their personal musings,
their genuine insights into their own life experiences.

That kind of spiritual journal became free space
where my soul could companion with others
who had dealt with the same kind of soul-stretching
questions
and hopes
that I had.

This daily dialogue
expanded my thinking beyond myself
but it also exposed me to myself, raw and searching.

It brought me
to look at spiritual questions and life issues
that plague us on a daily level—
however mundane, however troublesome.

The questions were so honest,
the topics so simple
that I began to realize that, in the end,
we are, each and all of us,
the real subject matter of the spiritual life.

But the value of it depends on the choice we make:

We can wend our way through life superficially,
questioning nothing and calling that faith,
repeating old platitudes,
numbing ourselves with old clichés.

Or we can choose to look at ourselves
in the very center of our souls,
admit the worst, however painful that may be,
but pursue the best hopes and ideals in us,

even when we are totally unsure
where the pursuit will take us.

I invite you to journal with me now,
to write your spiritual broodings down—
in all their simplicity,
in all their uncomfortable plainness.

To begin a spiritual journal that honestly faces
the person in the mirror
invites new insight into ourselves,
gives new meaning to our daily lives
and brings new life where only old ideas have been.

The spiritual life begins when we discover
that we only become spiritual adults
when we go beyond old answers to the root
of our questions,
when we go beyond our fear of uncertainty,
when we accept
the great encompassing mystery of life
that is God.

–Joan Chittister

* * *

"The things of the soul
must always be considered as
plentiful, spacious and large."

Teresa of Avila

_____

_____

_____

_____

_____

_____

_____

_____

Conversation 1

But what are "the things of the soul"? Surely they are every breath we breathe, every word we hear, every thought we think. The things of the soul have been too long compartmentalized. And so we got religion but not spirituality. We got church but not God. We got the sacred but not the sacredness of the secular. Or better yet, the revelation that there is nothing "secular" at all.

—Joan Chittister

_____

_____

_____

_____

_____

_____

_____

_____

* * *

"God is gracious and merciful…
slow to anger
and abounding in steadfast love."

Exodus 34:6

_____

_____

_____

_____

_____

_____

_____

_____

Conversation 2

Who is this God, really? Who is this God whom we have fashioned out of the light of our needs and the hopes of our hearts? When we are vengeful, we tell tall tales of an angry God. When we are sick with our own sin, we find ourselves a God of mercy. When we are pressed down, face in the sand, we know what a God of justice is all about. Is this God? Or is God the measure of how deep our smallness goes, how great our parching thirst for love? Surely God is all of this. And more. The more we cannot in our smallness and our thirst even begin to imagine.

–Joan Chittister

_____

_____

_____

_____

_____

_____

✳ ✳ ✳

When the death of their master was clearly imminent, the disciples became totally bereft. "If you leave us, Master," they pleaded, "how will we know what to do?" And the master replied, "I am nothing but a finger pointing at the moon. Perhaps when I am gone you will see the moon."

Sufi Tale

_____

_____

_____

_____

_____

_____

_____

_____

Conversation 3

The meaning is clear: It is God that religion must be about, not itself. When religion makes itself God, it ceases to be religion. But when religion becomes the bridge that leads to God, it stretches us to live to the limits of human possibility. It requires us to be everything we can possibly be: kind, generous, honest, loving, compassionate, just. It defines the standards of the human condition. It sets the parameters within which we direct our institutions. It provides the basis for the ethics that guide our human relationships. It sets out to enable us to be fully human, human beings.   –Joan Chittister

***

*"Spirituality is expressed
in everything we do."*

Anne E. Carr

Conversation 4

I believe that our lives are our spirituality but I am not sure that behavior is its best test, its certain indicator. I do a great many things that "look" good: I suppress anger, I give partial responses to serious questions, I hold myself to my own breast and live life within life within life that no one else knows about. But at the same time, I long desperately to bring all of them into focus, into line, into the One, where the heart is soft toward everything and everyone in this world. So which approach is real spirituality?

–Joan Chittister

* * *

"Mindfulness teaches us to be fully aware of each experience, letting nothing remain unnoticed, taking nothing for granted."

Holly Whitcomb

_____

_____

_____

_____

_____

_____

_____

_____

_____

Conversation 5

Mindfulness is the arch monastic virtue. Maybe that's why monastics choose small cells, unfrequented places, simple surroundings. After all, it can take a lifetime to really see flowers, feel wood, learn the sky, walk a path and hear what all these things are saying to us about life, about our own growth, about the spirit in the clay of us. But once mindfulness comes, life changes entirely.   –Joan Chittister

***

"It is through prayer...
that one will be given the most powerful light
to see God and self."

Angela of Foligno

_____

_____

_____

_____

_____

_____

_____

_____

_____

Conversation 6

"To see God" is to care very little about anything lesser. But in prayer I see my own littleness
most clearly. I know how cowardly I really am.
My voice is but one drop of water in an ocean of
oppression. It will not change the ocean. But it
may put it in need of explaining the injustice it
can no longer hide, perhaps. I cannot not speak
what my heart knows to be true.

–Joan Chittister

***

*"One of the marvelous facts of life
is that every ending carries within itself
the potential for a new beginning."*

Mary Borhek

_____

_____

_____

_____

_____

_____

_____

_____

_____

Conversation 7

I have had to learn this truth the hard way—and may not really have learned it at all. Whatever the public perception, I find it very difficult to give up the past. My pattern is to resist it kicking and screaming. But then, once the step is taken, never to look back. I simply am where I am—rooted until I go through the next forcible replanting—and then I root again. So far every planting has been a better one. When will I ever learn that?   –Joan Chittister

_____

_____

_____

_____

_____

_____

_____

* * *

"No one knows what lies ahead,
when we say yes to God."

Jan L. Richardson

_____

_____

_____

_____

_____

_____

_____

_____

_____

Conversation 8

I can only trust that what lies ahead will be fuller, freer, than the present. I hope for a life that is my own, that has no false chains to bind me, that allows me to move like a butterfly on the wind and to stand, when necessary, like a lioness in high grass. I want a life that is directed by the call within myself—not by an institution, not even by what looks like the care and concern of others.   –Joan Chittister

---

---

* * *

"The people who sat in darkness
have seen a great light."

Matthew 4:16

_____

_____

_____

_____

_____

_____

_____

_____

_____

_____

Conversation 9

Maybe one of the great unknown—unrecognized—truths of life is that light always dawns, eventually; that there is no such thing as a perpetual darkness of soul. I know that in my own case the darkness only existed because I refused the light. I simply did not want the light. I had been in the cocoon of darkness for so long I thought that it was light.

Maybe life is simply a going from light to light, from darkness to darkness till the last Great Darkness signals the coming of the First Great Light. That would explain why we are in a constant state of "disillusionment." I have come to understand that it is not protesting what we do not like that counts. It is choosing what we do which, ultimately, changes things.

–Joan Chittister

***

*"Love is the power
to act one another into well-being
and God is love."*

June Goudey

_____

_____

_____

_____

_____

_____

_____

_____

_____

Conversation 10

The people who love us prod us—enable us—to grow. And God loves us. Maybe that is why I have been moved from one nest to another, all the way through life: God loves me and wants me to grow. I am trying, before I die, to learn to trust this continual going into the unknown. I better have a long, long life.

—Joan Chittister

* * *

*"You shall worship the Sovereign your God,
and God only shall you serve."*

Matthew 4:10

_____

_____

_____

_____

_____

_____

_____

_____

_____

Conversation 11

These words trip off the tongue—all the while I worship other gods. Lesser genies of my ravenous soul. I have worshiped so many false gods in life, yet in the collapse of each of them—and they have indeed all collapsed—I have come closer, ironically, to the god who is God. Everything else has failed me—people, privilege, positions, profit—but not this God who is "not in the whirlwind." That God, like a magnet, draws me on. And someday, perhaps, I will lose myself down the black hole of nothingness and find everything. Without the dissatisfaction of the soul, how would we ever find our way to more?

–Joan Chittister

* * *

"We cannot afford not to fight
for growth and understanding,
even when it is painful,
as it is bound to be."

May Sarton

_____

_____

_____

_____

_____

_____

_____

_____

Conversation 12

When we grow enough to understand that we are at a dead end, then what? Is it time to be resigned or time to struggle for breath, for new life, with all our might? I always thought that life got quieter, more settled, happier as time went on. But that's not true. On the contrary. We simply become more aware of what we've missed, what we've given ourselves to that was not worth the giving. –Joan Chittister

_____

_____

_____

_____

_____

_____

_____

_____

***

*"In the beginning was the Word
and the Word was with God
and the Word was God."*

John 1:1

_____

_____

_____

_____

_____

_____

_____

_____

Conversation 13

This week I will start a new book. I live in hope of the living Word in it. I also listen for the word of my own life that is true. Is it simply to go on, to finish what I began simply because I began it? Or is it to become what's missing, whatever the upheaval it will cost me. That is the major question of my life right now. I long to put down the institution, the definition, the responsibilities, the expectations, the connections. I long to begin over . . . to become silence . . . to disappear. —Joan Chittister

_____

_____

_____

_____

_____

_____

_____

* * *

*"When the Spirit of Truth comes
we shall experience freedom,
set free from all that has closed us in."*

Mercy Oduyoye

_____

_____

_____

_____

_____

_____

_____

_____

Conversation 14

We are all so closed in and we don't even know it: by our language, by our cultures, by our religions, by our sex, by our age. So how can we possibly expect that we know God? I feel as if my life has been spent straining to see through a knothole the size of a pinhead into a dark room. But when we even begin to see, the breadth of the view breaks open the heart.

–Joan Chittister

_____

_____

_____

_____

_____

_____

_____

_____

***

"Set your minds on things that are above,
not on things that are on earth."

Colossians 3:2

_____

_____

_____

_____

_____

_____

_____

_____

Conversation 15

All my life my mind has been "set on things that are above." And as a result, the me that is in need of freedom and life and joy and unlimited possibility and love has languished. Been ignored. Suppressed. And now, on the brink of the grave, that me is crying for attention. Is this unfinished business — or temptation? Is it an opportunity, a "call" or a snare? Is it a lesser life or the rest of life? And how will I ever know if I should have continued the journey or stay fixed in a system on the way to dust. Where are you, O God, in this?   –Joan Chittister

_____

_____

_____

_____

_____

_____

***

*"But Jesus came and touched them, saying,
'Rise and have no fear.'"*

Matthew 17:7

_____

_____

_____

_____

_____

_____

_____

_____

_____

Conversation 16

I wonder what it takes to really "rise and have no fear"? I have a great deal of fear sometimes. I fear that I will do poorly what I want to do well. I fear that I have done all the wrong things in life, made all the wrong choices. I fear being trapped by other people's expectations. I fear grinding my life away in the great institutional sacrifice—for which there is no final sense, and even little present purpose. I watch religious life and fear that it was the wrong thing to have done in the first place and yet—even knowing how poorly I've done it—I know it was not. And in the core of me, as a result, I really do "have no fear."   –Joan Chittister

* * *

"Those who find their life will lose it,
and those who lose their life for my sake
will find it."

Matthew 10:39

_____

_____

_____

_____

_____

_____

_____

_____

_____

_____

Conversation 17

Whatever we do, we do for a purpose larger than ourselves or there is no use doing it at all. The real purpose of our lives is not for ourselves alone. It is to co-create the world. It is to bring the rest of the world to the point of humanity we think ourselves to have achieved. It is when all I care about is my life that I begin to have it seep out of me into a pool of selfishness so deep that I miss the juice of all the life that is around me.　　　　　　　　　　–Joan Chittister

* * *

*"Reflect on your times of busyness
and preoccupation, times when you
possibly resist God's presence."*

Wendy Miller

_____

_____

_____

_____

_____

_____

_____

_____

_____

Conversation 18

I am never closer to God than in the moments when I am busiest. It is in those times that I throw myself on the mind of God and listen to know if the direction is right, if the words are right, if the ideas are right. Then God becomes the radar by which I steer. I stray farthest from the consciousness of God when I relax and coast. Then I take God for granted.

–Joan Chittister

_____

_____

_____

_____

_____

_____

_____

_____

* * *

"Take my yoke upon you and learn from me
for I am gentle and lowly of heart
and you will find rest for your souls."

Matthew 11:29

_____

_____

_____

_____

_____

_____

_____

_____

_____

Conversation 19

The message is a clear one: being gentle and humble is a spiritual posture that is good for mental health. When I am given to anger or driven by the kind of pride that fears failure and resists defeat, I doom myself to eternal agitation. I manufacture my own anguish. When I demand that the world take the shape I decide for it, when I get frustrated at airline counters and impatient with my computer, I insist on waging eternal contest with life. Then I have the nerve to wonder how the world got dedicated to violence? Then I wonder why I have no peace. The truth is that the upheavals all started with me. The spiritual equation is obvious: exterior calm leads to internal quiet.   –Joan Chittister

_____

_____

_____

_____

_____

_____

✳ ✳ ✳

"Some people esteem one day as better than another, while others esteem all days alike. Let all be fully convinced in their own mind."

Romans 14:5

_____

_____

_____

_____

_____

_____

_____

_____

_____

Conversation 20

Life is a matter of attitude. It becomes what we bring to it. I find myself vacillating between the very poles Paul describes. At pole one, I take the position that this particular thing is good but this other thing is bad. So my days are either wonderful or terrible depending on whether they take the shape I will for them. At pole two, I take the position that everything that happens is life-giving somehow, even when I can't see how. Then God is in the crevices where I never thought to look. "Make up your mind," Paul seems to say, "and it will change your whole life."

–Joan Chittister

* * *

"What is essential for taking back a yesterday
is understanding that you are not alone,
even in the wilderness."

Linda H. Hollies

_____

_____

_____

_____

_____

_____

_____

_____

_____

Conversation 21

Knowing that someone else knows where you are, feels the way you feel, does—for me at least—really "take back yesterday." It smoothes whatever scars were suffered there. It is being alone in my pain, my fear, the burden of my memories, that presses my face to the ground. But when one person says, "I know," . . ."I understand," . . ."I can see why you feel that way," I become whole again. Sane. Mature. It is the humanity of the other that brings my humanity back to life.   –Joan Chittister

* * *

*"When we have friends and really
share our truth with them, it changes
the way things are from the inside out."*

Donna Schaper

_____

_____

_____

_____

_____

_____

_____

_____

_____

Conversation 22

I strive for truth but never really achieve it with anyone, because I fear hurting them, disillusioning them, scandalizing them, depressing them. I would love to be "truthful" with someone but I am beginning to doubt that that's really possible for anyone. In fact, is it even fair to burden the other with a "truth" that can't be changed? Maybe the most we can achieve is honesty about our questions.   –Joan Chittister

_____

_____

_____

_____

_____

_____

_____

_____

* * *

*"Genuine wisdom involves learning
from the wisdoms of other forgotten
or overlooked people."*

Maria Harris

_____

_____

_____

_____

_____

_____

_____

_____

_____

Conversation 23

As we get older—or at least as I am getting older, more aware of the sound of death at my back—I find myself watching other people with great intensity. I want to know what they know about living well. I want to hear from them what they now regret. I want to sift and pan the gold of every moment that is slipping away from me sleek and empty.   –Joan Chittister

_____

_____

_____

_____

_____

_____

_____

_____

* * *

*"When has someone's
honest and caring listening enabled you
to express and transform your anger?"*

Jan L. Richardson

_____

_____

_____

_____

_____

_____

_____

_____

_____

Conversation 24

Listeners are life's rarest breed. Parent figures, gurus, commanders, curial overlords, and nags are easy to come by. Listeners—those who hear the pain behind the pain, allow you to probe it, and work with you to find a way beyond it—come few and far between. In all my life, I have known only two. But they have made all the difference. Thanks to them I have survived both my beginnings and my endings.

                                              –Joan Chittister

_____

_____

_____

_____

_____

_____

_____

_____

***

*"Pray, therefore, to the Sovereign of the harvest
to send out laborers into the fields."*

Matthew 9:38

_____

_____

_____

_____

_____

_____

_____

_____

_____

Conversation 25

It is not my responsibility to save the world, to stop the war, to change the church, to liberate women. God will see to all of that because planetary destruction, government-sponsored slaughter—for which "war" is a pornographic euphemism—ecclesiastical imperialism, and sexism are all insidious worms inside otherwise great ideas. But it is my responsibility to do something to eradicate each of them from where I stand or bear the sin of being part of all of them. Consciousness commits. Once I see that what calls itself virtue is really sin, I have no choice but to resist it. But, the end of it all depends on society's being able to achieve a critical mass of resistance. For that, God will need to "send out laborers into the field."

–Joan Chittister

_____

_____

_____

_____

_____

* * *

"Each of us constructs a life
that is her own central metaphor
for thinking about the world."

Mary Catherine Bateson

_____

_____

_____

_____

_____

_____

_____

_____

Conversation 26

My metaphor for thinking about the world is "The Beloved of God." It means that I must tie my life to the voice of God in my heart as I hear it through the poor, the oppressed, the disenfranchised, and those with voices other than the voice of the institutions. For that I may be rejected by the system, of course, but I cannot keep my soul and do otherwise.

–Joan Chittister

***

"For this is our God
and we are the people of God's pasture
and the sheep of God's hand."

Psalm 95:7

_____

_____

_____

_____

_____

_____

_____

_____

Conversation 27

It is sometimes very difficult to know where God is for us: in the demands of authority for obedience to the sins they call virtue—for the nonordination of women, for instance—in the name of "unity." Or is God in the questions of the heart that deserve to be pursued—that demand to be answered—in the light of the rest of the gospel. And so the question haunts me: Would Jesus stay in the church today? In any of them? And, if not, who would follow him out of it? Would I? Yes, there's the question. I have lived a lifetime of ecclesiastical sins: no "mixed marriages," they taught, and then changed their minds; no burial for fetuses; no moral absolutes about wife beating; no protection of Jews; no resistance to segregation. And I went along with all of them.

—Joan Chittister

✳ ✳ ✳

"Do not be conformed to this world,
but be transformed
by the renewal of your mind."

Romans 12:2

_____

_____

_____

_____

_____

_____

_____

_____

_____

Conversation 28

Exactly how does a person go about not being "conformed to this world"? We live in the belly of the beast. It is our politicians, our banks, our businesses that cheat poor laborers, make the dirty military alliances, sell the weapons, hike up the interest rates. And we are the ones who buy from them, and elect them, and collect their dividends. Is there any hope for our own purity of soul in such a world as this? Is there any hope for mine? Well, Paul seems to think so. He says, "Be transformed by the renewal of your mind." Change the way you think, in other words. And say so. That's what I must do. Whatever the ridicule, whatever the criticism, I must say so. Loudly, clearly, always. Then maybe someday I will find myself lost in a chorus of voices all shouting "no" together. And then the world will change.   –Joan Chittister

***

*"Gifts of the heart
are what memories are made of."*

Sheryl Nicholson

_____

_____

_____

_____

_____

_____

_____

_____

Conversation 29

I have a theory that only what touches the heart is really lodged in the mind. Memory is made up of what has touched our lives. So, in later years, the data drops away because it is useless. But soft touches, hard words, deep joys, great pain never leave us. For good or ill, they remain. They are always there, soothing us or torturing our souls. The life question it leaves us with may be worth thinking about, What do we do with the feelings that clog our souls?

–Joan Chittister

✳ ✳ ✳

That which is born of the flesh is flesh,
and that which is born of the Spirit is spirit.

John 3:6

_____

_____

_____

_____

_____

_____

_____

_____

Conversation 30

What does it mean to be "born of the flesh" and "born of the spirit" and in the end does it really make any difference? So much in me "born of the flesh"—done to satisfy my appetites—has in the end changed my spirit. And many times for the good. And those things in me "born of the spirit"—meant to be idealistic, "spiritual"— have just as many times been corrupting. I was a "good Catholic" and so became disdainful of those who weren't Catholic. How unholy can a person be? So now I suspect the separation of flesh and spirit and am open to both. That way, perhaps someday holiness will sneak in when I'm not looking.   –Joan Chittister

_____

_____

_____

_____

_____

_____

***

"Change is the manifestation of our ability
to grow and become."

Anne Wilson Schaef

_____

_____

_____

_____

_____

_____

_____

_____

_____

Conversation 31

I am still becoming: I am becoming myself—independent, different, free. Those are dangerous, unacceptable, qualities. They violate groupness. And yet, without this kind of change, can we possibly die adults? My problem is that this kind of change came so late and more in response to rejection than to process. But whatever the circumstances, the leap was worth it. I am not the person I was before. I am changed forever.
                                                    –Joan Chittister

_____

_____

_____

_____

_____

_____

_____

***

"Keep traveling, Sister! Keep traveling!
The road is far from finished."

Nelle Morton

_____

_____

_____

_____

_____

_____

_____

_____

Conversation 32

Indeed we are not finished. The struggle for women is only just begun actually. But I have come to the conclusion that social change does not happen in a straight line. It's run and coast, run and coast all the way. This is another deceleration period, perhaps. Everything has quieted, slowed for a while, no big demonstrations, no great amount of organizing. But it is precisely now that we must not stop or we will stand to lose our hearts along the way.

                                            –Joan Chittister

***

"Springtime God . . .
we need your persistent love to disturb . . .
our heart's rigidity."

Kate Compston

_____

_____

_____

_____

_____

_____

_____

_____

_____

Conversation 33

I love the image of a "springtime God."
Isn't God always in the growing season in us?
Isn't everything that happens in life simply
seeding something to come—and isn't all of it
God? But if that's true, the question is, then, Are
all our thoughts new seeds of life to be pursued?
Because if so, then I am being called on and I
am, as usual, reluctant to go.   –Joan Chittister

_____

_____

_____

_____

_____

_____

_____

_____

* * *

"A wisdom still abides in the natural rhythms of the earth, if we are still and open ourselves to it."

Kimberly Greene Angle

_____

_____

_____

_____

_____

_____

_____

_____

_____

Conversation 34

There is a wisdom in natural rhythm but we long ago abandoned it to technology and electricity. Now there is no stopping, no ending. Only quitting. I long ago fell prey to it and forgot how to stop and wondered how to quit. So now two unnatural rhythms try for the marrow of my soul: fatigue that is chronic and frustration that is terminal. I am determined to defeat them both.

My God is definitely a God of the seasons. I prefer that God in spring and fall—when things emerge and things mellow—but I have learned more from the God who is the heat of my day and the icy obstacles of my life. From that God I have learned the depths of the self.

–Joan Chittister

* * *

"It is through our human experience
that we meet God."

Elaine Ward

_____

_____

_____

_____

_____

_____

_____

_____

_____

_____

Conversation 35

It takes a lifetime to really understand that God is in what is standing in front of us. Most of our lives are spent looking, straining to see the God in the cloud, behind the mist, beyond the dark. It is when we face God in one another, in creation, in the moment, that the real spiritual journey begins.

–Joan Chittister

* * *

"God restores my soul.
God leads me in paths of righteousness
for God's name's sake.

Psalm 23:3

_____

_____

_____

_____

_____

_____

_____

_____

Conversation 36

When I am feeling battered by life—sometimes even by life at its best—I take a deep breath and remember that though God is in all of it, God is also greater than all of it. Then both what I lose in the battering and what I become because of it are simply chances to be more of the real thing, to become more than the thing itself. At the end of everything is God.

–Joan Chittister

* * *

"When the mundane things that occupy our time threaten to dull our view of the universe, it is time to slow down."

Madeline McClenney-Sadler

_____

_____

_____

_____

_____

_____

_____

_____

Conversation 37

The "mundane" is certainly dull, I agree, and may even limit us — not only our perceptions but even the breadth of our questions. At the same time, there is something very freeing, very humanizing about the mundane. Doing dishes and buying vegetables get us back in touch with ourselves, give us time to smell the earth of our lives, give us time just to be. We will go on long after the big ideas fade and the profession ends. The question is, Will there be anything in me then? Will there be a me in me? It all depends on how I deal with the mundane.

–Joan Chittister

***

*"God makes me to lie down in green pastures
and leads me beside still waters."*

Psalm 23:2

_____

_____

_____

_____

_____

_____

_____

_____

_____

Conversation 38

I have to believe this scripture fiercely right now because life does not feel like "green pastures" or "still water." It feels like a living death. Everyone around me is still producing, still building, still going on. But I am cut off at the root with nothing to show for it. I am empty, useless, doing nothing, going nowhere. The speeches and the books flash and fade and I am embarrassed by my existence. So where is God in all of this? What is life without life? I feel like I am on the other side of a window pane looking in and no one sees me. No one is unkind; they are simply uncaring. It is "make your own way time" . . . and I don't know how.

–Joan Chittister

* * *

"All through the long winter
I dream of my garden.
On the first warm day of spring
I dig my fingers deep into the soft earth . . .
and my spirits soar."

Helen Hayes

_____

_____

_____

_____

_____

_____

_____

_____

Conversation 39

I never dream of gardens but I do dream of keyboards and dogs and water. They are all the things that give me back myself. I sink into them and all the irritations drain away. I become then who I really am and I become deliriously happy. I become untethered from expectations and agendas and responsibilities. I become—I feel—truly whole. The spiritual discipline to be developed at a time of great pressure is to do more of the things that soak our spirits in laughter and smiles. But how? The dog is gone; the water is gone. And the keyboard intrudes on the life of others. However, there is always memory —and always hope.

–Joan Chittister

* * *

"The wastelands of life around us
cannot shut out
the promise of life-giving water."

Lavon Bayler

_____

_____

_____

_____

_____

_____

_____

_____

Conversation 40

There is that within us that shouts always, "more." As far as I'm concerned, this is our single greatest proof of the existence of God. It seems that we are born with a memory in our hearts of where we've been and consciousness of where we're going—and nothing else satisfies along the way.　　　　　－Joan Chittister

_____

_____

_____

_____

_____

_____

_____

_____

_____